to you

silver

22/03/15

i dreamt today.
she was there. in a room. with someone.
i left my grey sweater on the floor. water leaked and ruined it. it became heavy and large and jealous.

31/03/15

1:42 AM

how do you feel today?

i feel awful

01/04/15

spring soon

i've spoken to the people in my head and we've decided it would be a good time to start living with an exhilarating intensity.

i'll be out of breath by summer.

the metroman spoke through the interphone but everything he said sounded muffled and sibylline, maybe he announced the imminent explosion of the train. death could be a couple seconds away.
i wouldn't know.
i couldn't hear.

07/04/15

i was semi-passively looking for you

i owe her a story.

have we shared enough moments to properly fall in love?

i knew nothing

you know what's the best part

about this?

i'm sure it wont be weird after

people hate awkwardness

08/04/15

i can't die in my dreams
but i like to think:
our love is real

kissing you

slicing a throat

15/04/15

it's been a while
i've been dreaming a lot.
don't worry.
i've saved them elsewhere
in my memory and that of others
places unsafe where they will be forgotten

i also tried suggestion to attain

a handless orgasm

it sort of worked

i felt light and heavy

pinned down and lifted up

i'll try it again soon

she had a migraine

i suggested she massage her inner

thumb like Dr. Oz taught me

she said it worked

i'm happy because my next remedy

was an orgasm and i'm not sure

how close we are.

2 years

of mandatory solitude

03/05/15

what day is it?

the past week has been

sans time

sans watch

sans phone

08/05/15

i keep losing things

saying things is harder

than you think

the trade-off between scarcity
and abundance is odd in the world
of words
these days, people navigate
between terse and prolix speech
in phases of opaque mystery and
transparent narcissism

09/06/15

i'm on dog duty

14/06/15

she made a pie-chart
for her life

15/06/15

it's not hard to imagine a successful black man. it's much harder imagining one dating your white daughter.

22/07/15

the beauty of that beat

is that it never truly drops

- watch out

13/08/15

nightmares of losing you
wide awake
you've never been everything
you're more than another pair of eyes
i won't stand to be alone on tuesday nights
i may have to start going out again

this is a premature eulogy
can someone get between my gun and my foot?

13/08/15

as long as it's easy
it'll work
don't make this complicated
don't get your heart or your brain
into this
don't ask for ties and ropes
they'll bring your demise
then you'll want to hang yourself
with them

13/08/15

nothing about you is special
why do i care so much?
i only care when i'm alone
when my mind imagines your death
you're only alive when you're with me
that's why i don't watch your snapchats
you're only alive when you're with me

13/08/15

don't take this the wrong way
but you're the only one i think about
maybe you won
it'll probably be a lose-lose

13/08/15

i made these 4 poems

4 months before your birthday

if these words make it through the fall

i owe you an apology

today

i don't owe you an apology
i was right
on the night of your birthday
you told me
there was someone else
because what else was i to expect
i woke up next to you
alone
i stopped speaking to you
i went on with my life
blessed with cursed premonitions

shadows

i waited for the train

always at the same spot

right between orange coat guy

and the small crevice on the floor

i had this plan

that the eight minutes we spent every morning together

would turn into a lifetime

that she would fall in love with me

bit by bit

like poison in a king's meal

i lay in bed

next to my phone

as if it were you

sometimes i feel like typing your name

in the facebook search-bar

i did

i saw you

your face

your dog

your boyfriend

your moon tattoo

our nine mutual friends

sometimes i feel like typing you name

in the facebook search-bar

and clicking the add friend button

to see what would happen

to remember why you deleted me

i feel lame writing about you
after almost ten years

but i did think about you today
genuinely
i remember the feeling of joy
waking up from sleepless nights
texting you
i remembered what it felt like
being 14 and in love

i remembered what it felt like

being 14 and in love

hoping you would come over

that friday my parents were gone

things would have been so much easier
had we been neighbors

our messages lay in a virtual graveyard
on app that no longer exists

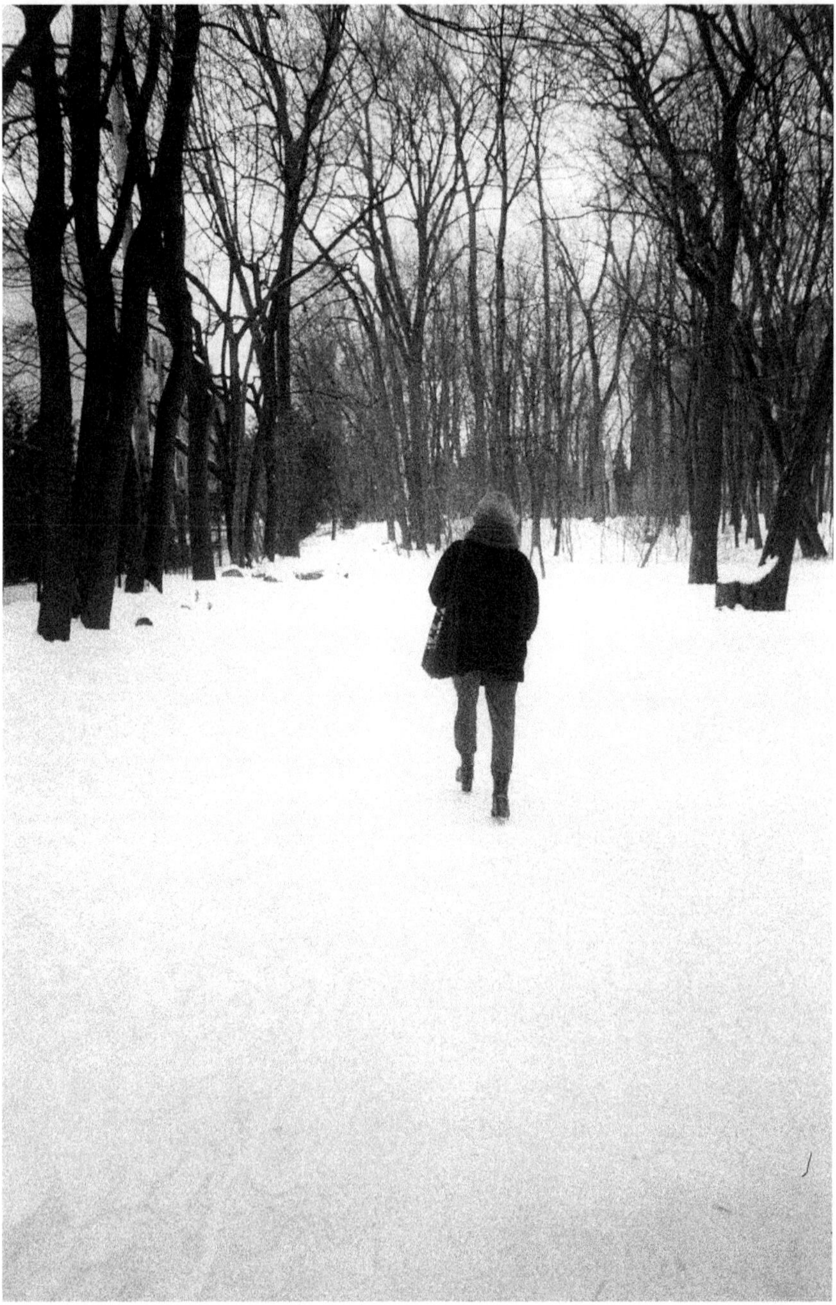

crimes

i'm a little ball

of self-absorbed shit

forgive me mom and dad

once again

you were right

all along

the first thing i did

when i came back

was leave you

a couple steps away: sleep

swallow down the vial

until empty

lay calm

in the sheets my mother washed

i try to avoid

feeling like shit about myself

i stopped drinking this year

there's a lot of things i stopped doing

this year

like chasing happiness

i figured

if i play hard-to-get

maybe

it'll text me first

eulogy #2

she ran away

and married a mountain

she understands

what it's like

being in love

with a thousand frozen rocks

sometimes

i want to leave everything

my job

my country

even you

to go back

and build

a million skyscrapers

words slip out of my mouth

like blossoming snakes

always poisonous

you're my favorite morning cartoon

every boy i hate

will find a loving wife

no luck

no fate

no gods

i'm just a couple keystrokes on a word document

there's a wild rabbit

in my neighbourhood

i see it when i come home alone

i can't stop thinking about you

you probably think i'm duller

than the common kitchen spoon

i got the pictures

with no return address

thank you

i wish we had the kind of memories
we could share over a meal
not the kind you send by mail
but then again
that's entirely my fault

i still have your book

the one by brauntigan

with your favorite poems highlighted

i wish i could give it back to you

i can only read "coke"

so many times

how quick the snow is to disappear

how quick they are to never text again

the petals become crunchy

they shrivel up and twist

like frozen dancers

your favorite season must be summer

let's watch cartoons

and fall asleep

dreaming of death

rather be with you

than alone

in another stranger's bed

my afternoon naps

teemed with dreams of you

i woke up bitter

a thousand dollars away from you

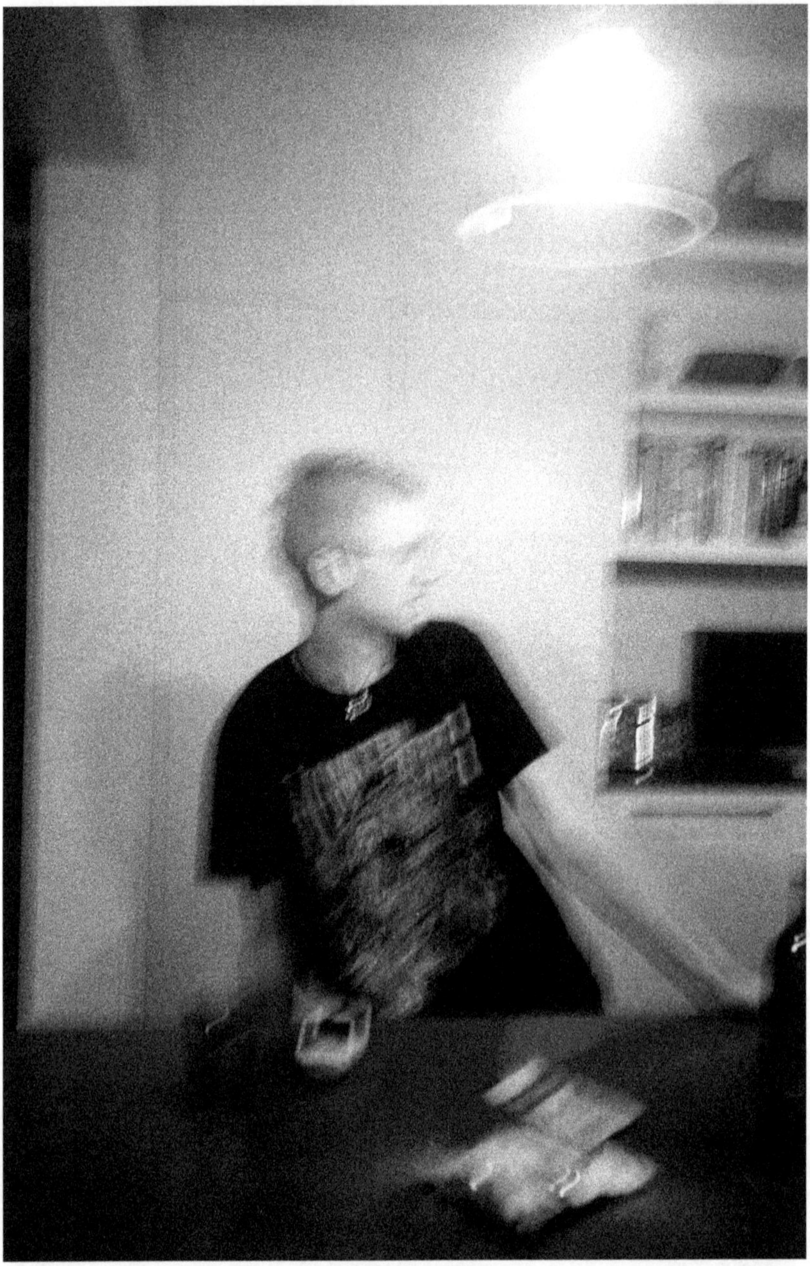

moon

i'm sorry

i couldn't stand myself.

i went outside

and i burnt

my shoes

my socks

my pants

my shirt

my skin

my eyes

my hands

unworthy of all these things

i even jumped in the fire

but my memory was too heavy and wet

it couldn't burn

i left the air steamy with self-disgust

the luxury of oblivion

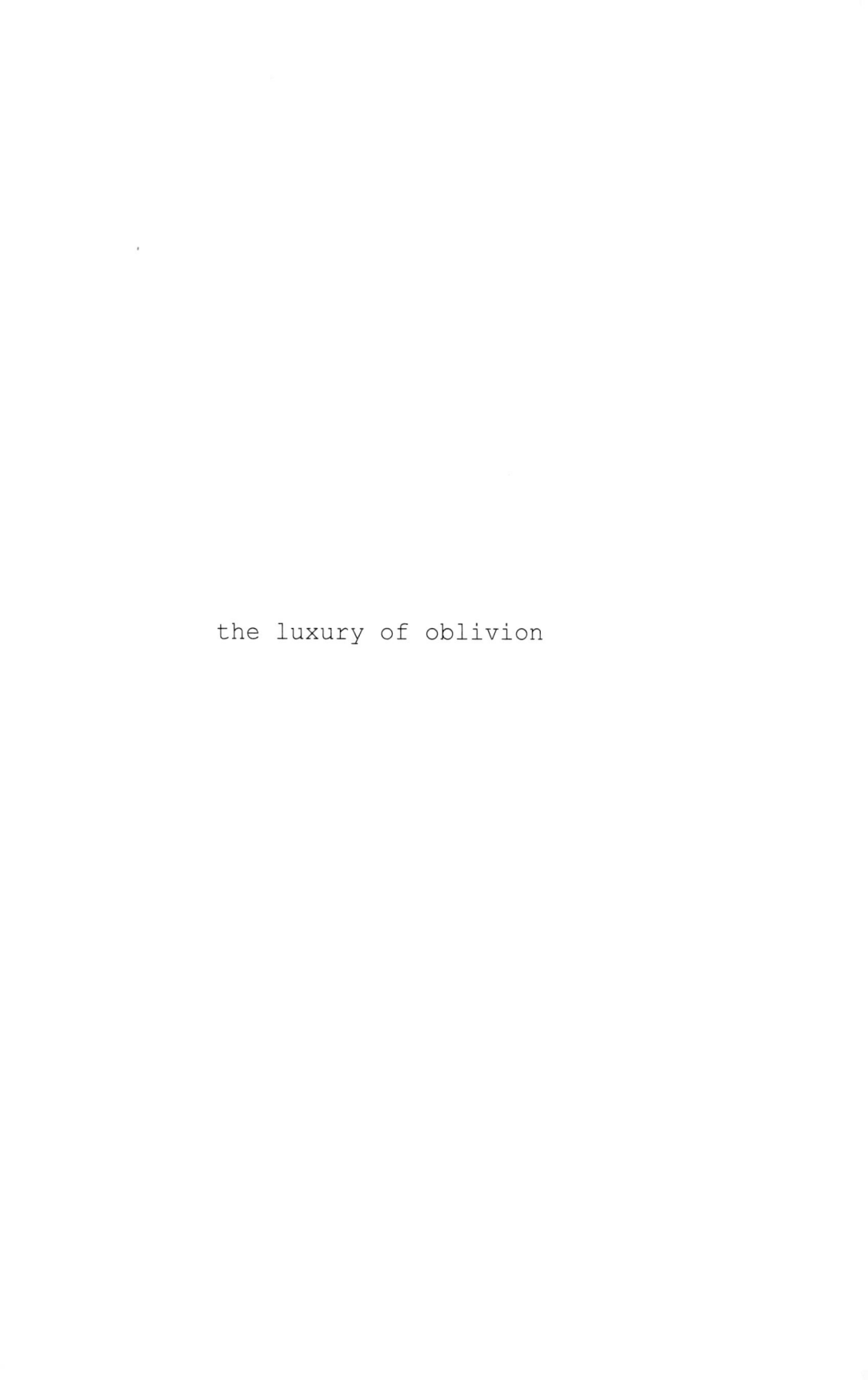

ON BLACKNESS

YOU CANNOT TELL ME HOW TO LIVE MY BLACKNESS
IT IS MINE
NO ONE DEFINES WHAT IT IS TO BE BLACK
I DO
MUST I LOOK LIKE THE PEOPLE YOU SEE ON TV
LIKE WHAT THE FUCK DO YOU KNOW ABOUT BEING BLACK
EVERYTIME
I FEEL INSULTED
I FEEL VIOLATED
I GET PISSED
IMAGINE
TO BE TOLD THAT YOU'RE FAILING AT BEING YOUR-SELF
THAT THE ONE THING THAT SOCIETY PUTS YOU DOWN FOR
THE ONE THING YOU TRY TO TAKE PRIDE IN
THE FIRST THING PEOPLE SEE ABOUT YOU
THE FIRST THING PEOPLE SAY ABOUT YOU
THAT YOU'RE NOT REALLY THAT
ACTUALLY, YOU'RE PRETTY "WHITE"
"YOU'RE AN OREO"
"BLACK OUTSIDE, WHITE INSIDE"
YOU DRESS FANCY
YOU WENT TO PRIVATE SCHOOL
YOU SPEAK RIGHT
YOU TALK SMART
AS IF THOSE AREN'T BLACK?
WHAT IS?
THE LOUDNESS IN THE BUS?
THE WEAVES?
THE FUNNY INTERNET VIDEOS?
HIPHOP?
SAGGING PANTS?

THE GANG VIOLENCE?
THE HIGHEST INCARCERAL RATE?
THE BLOOD ON MY ANCESTORS' CLOTHES?
THE POVERTY IN MY HOME COUNTRY?
MY GRANDPARENTS' ILLITERACY?
THE CONSTANT FIGHT FOR IDENTITY?
THE CONSTANT FIGHT FOR FREEDOM?
ROSA IN THE BUS?
MARTIN IN SELMA?
EVERY SINGLE DAY OF MY GOD FORSAKEN LIFE?

IS THAT NOT BLACK?
IS THAT NOT BLACK ENOUGH?
MUST I SHOW YOU THE MARKS ON MY WRISTS?
MUST I SHOW YOU THE MARKS ON MY WRISTS?
MUST I SHOW YOU THE MARKS ON MY WRISTS?
FROM THE SHACKLES
FROM THE HANDCUFFS
FROM THE –
MUST I SHOW YOU THE TEARS IN MY FACE AS I WRITE THESE WORDS?
BECAUSE IN THIS QUEST FOR MY IDENTITY
IN THESE TWENTY YEARS OF SOUL SEARCHING
I HAVEN'T FOUND A THING

BECAUSE A HUNDRED YEARS AGO I DIDN'T HAVE ONE

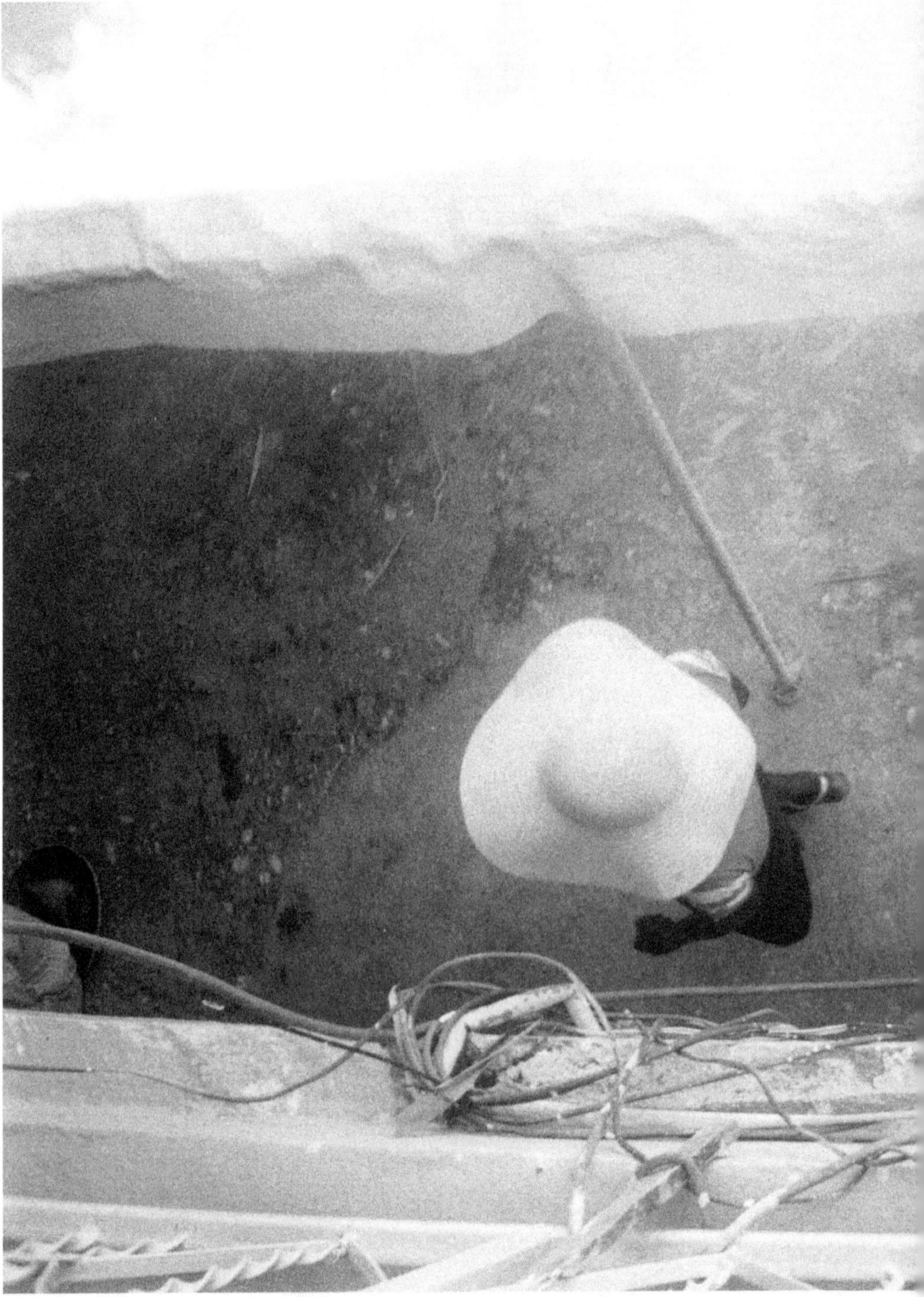

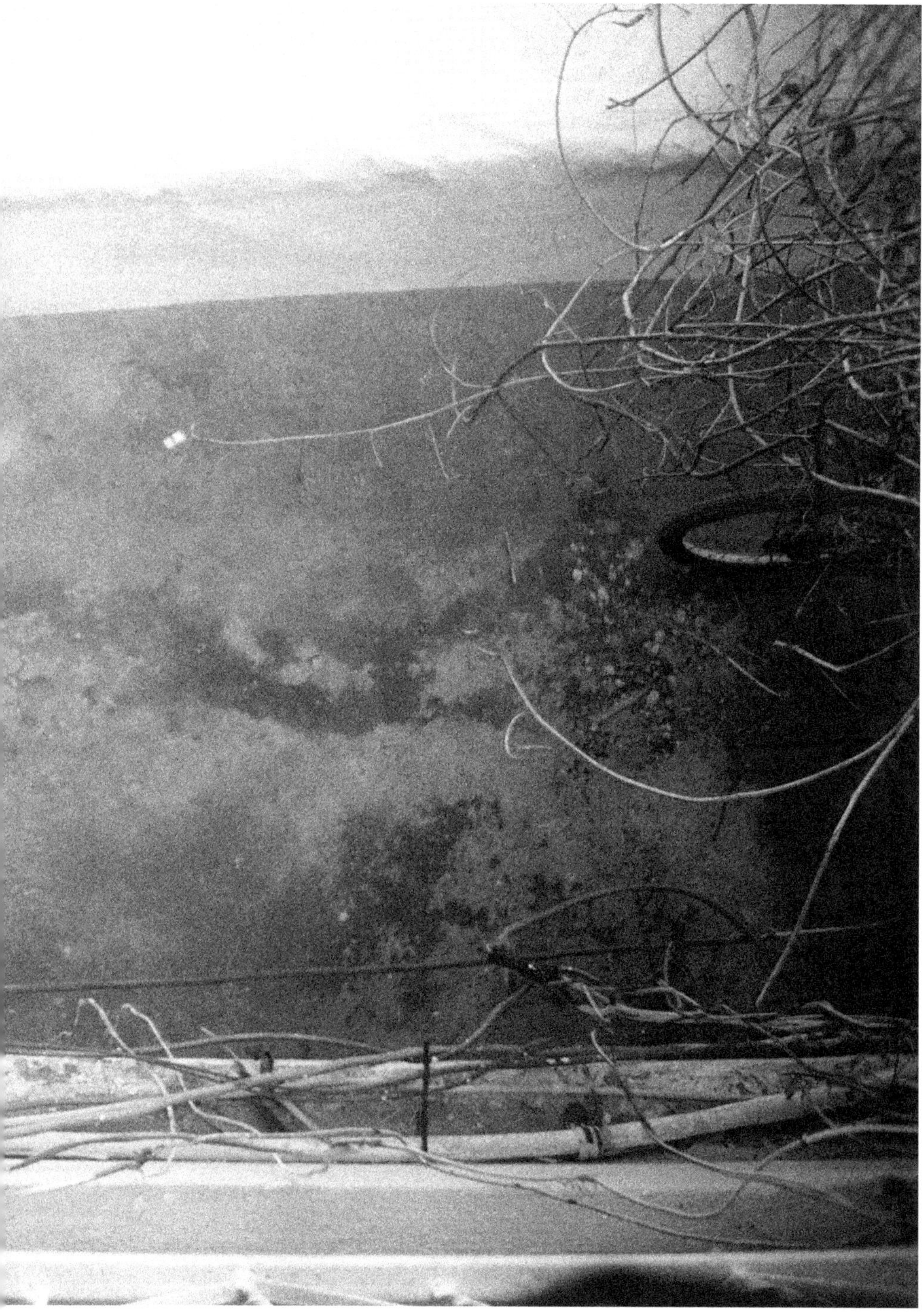

i should go

i should go

promise you'll keep this between you and me, it's terribly hard being honest
promise you'll keep this between you and me, it's terribly hard being honest
promise you'll keep this between you and me, it's terribly hard being honest
promise you'll keep this between you and me, it's terribly hard being honest
promise you'll keep this between you and me, it's terribly hard being honest
promise you'll keep this between you and me, it's terribly hard being honest
promise you'll keep this between you and me, it's terribly hard being honest
promise you'll keep this between you and me, it's terribly hard being honest
promise you'll keep this between you and me, it's terribly hard being honest
promise you'll keep this between you and me, it's terribly hard being honest
promise you'll keep this between you and me, it's terribly hard being honest
promise you'll keep this between you and me, it's terribly hard being honest
promise you'll keep this between you and me, it's terribly hard being honest
promise you'll keep this between you and me, it's terribly hard being honest
promise you'll keep this between you and me, it's terribly hard being honest
promise you'll keep this between you and me, it's terribly hard being honest
promise you'll keep this between you and me, it's terribly hard being honest
promise you'll keep this between you and me, it's terribly hard being honest
promise you'll keep this between you and me, it's terribly hard being honest
promise you'll keep this between you and me, it's terribly hard being honest
promise you'll keep this between you and me, it's terribly hard being honest
promise you'll keep this between you and me, it's terribly hard being honest
promise you'll keep this between you and me, it's terribly hard being honest
promise you'll keep this between you and me, it's terribly hard being honest
promise you'll keep this between you and me, it's terribly hard being honest
promise you'll keep this between you and me, it's terribly hard being honest
promise you'll keep this between you and me, it's terribly hard being honest
promise you'll keep this between you and me, it's terribly hard being honest
promise you'll keep this between you and me, it's terribly hard being honest
promise you'll keep this between you and me, it's terribly hard being honest
promise you'll keep this between you and me, it's terribly hard being honest
promise you'll keep this between you and me, it's terribly hard being honest
promise you'll keep this between you and me, it's terribly hard being honest
promise you'll keep this between you and me, it's terribly hard being honest
promise you'll keep this between you and me, it's terribly hard being honest
promise you'll keep this between you and me, it's terribly hard being honest
promise you'll keep this between you and me, it's terribly hard being honest
promise you'll keep this between you and me, it's terribly hard being honest
promise you'll keep this between you and me, it's terribly hard being honest
promise you'll keep this between you and me, it's terribly hard being honest
promise you'll keep this between you and me, it's terribly hard being honest
promise you'll keep this between you and me, it's terribly hard being honest
promise you'll keep this between you and me, it's terribly hard being honest

CPSIA information can be obtained
at www.ICGtesting.com
Printed in the USA
LVHW081516140219
607560LV00032B/968/P